THE WORLD GOT SICK WITH A VIRUS

The Pandemic of 2020

by

Adira J. Parker

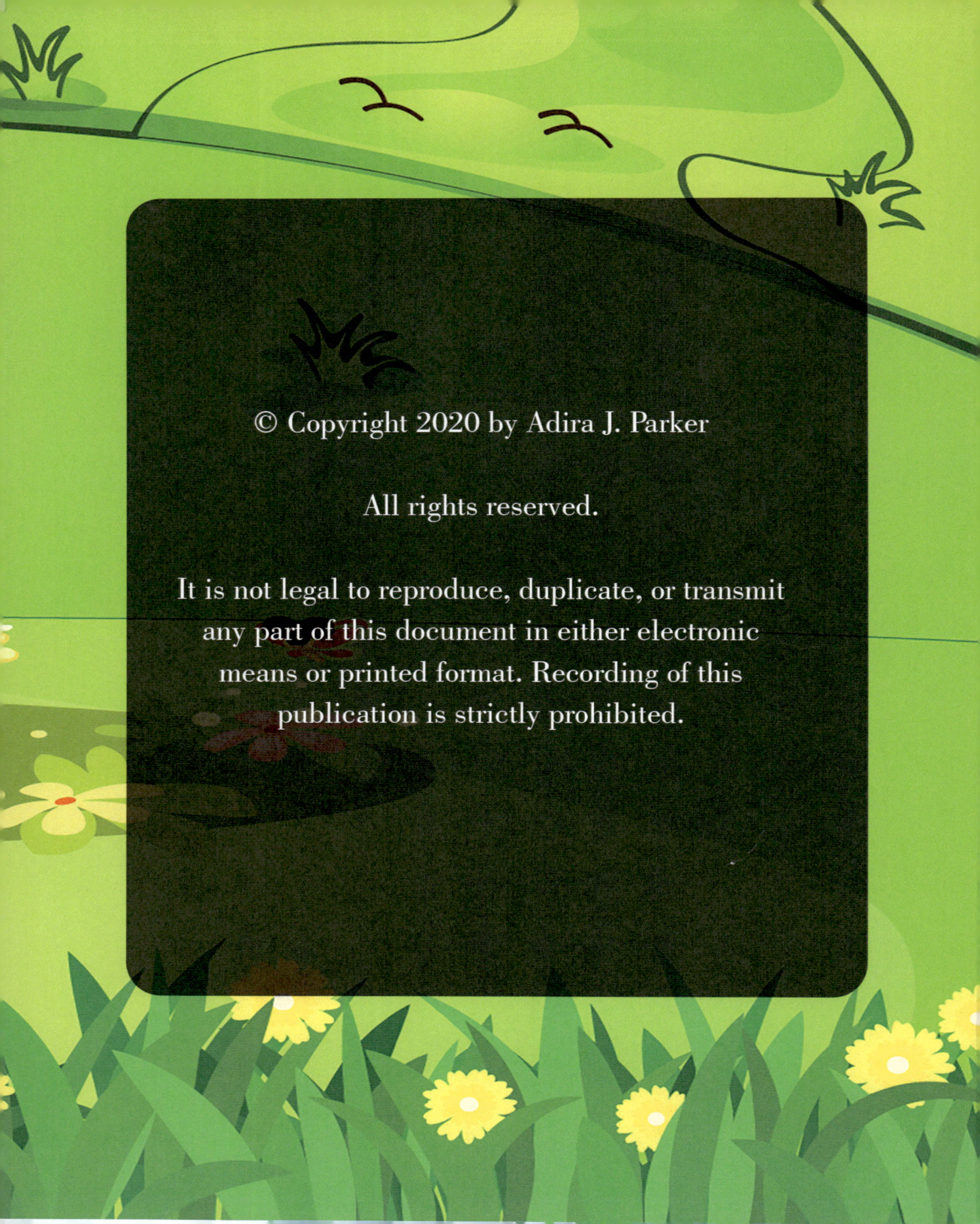

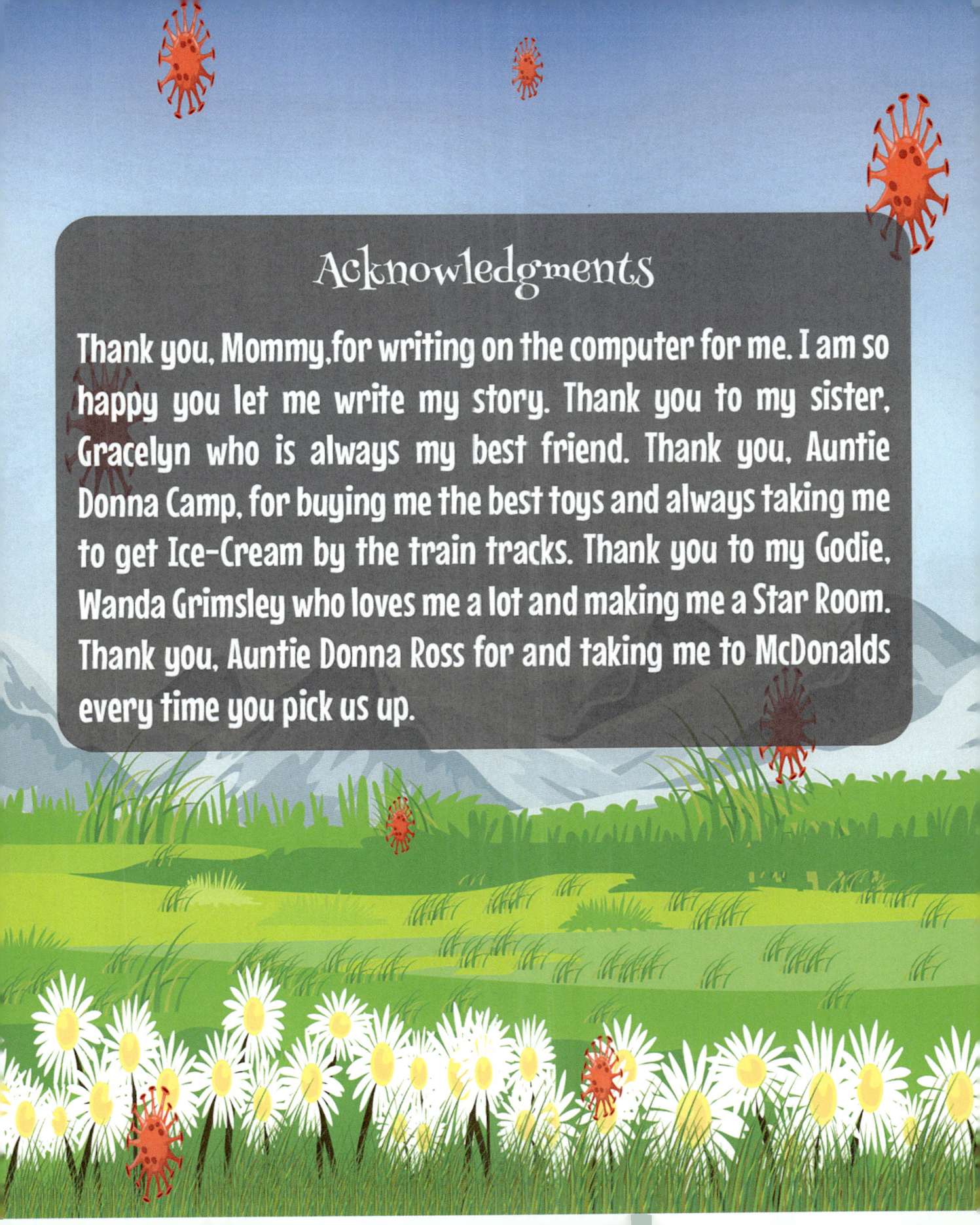

Acknowledgments

Thank you, Mommy, for writing on the computer for me. I am so happy you let me write my story. Thank you to my sister, Gracelyn who is always my best friend. Thank you, Auntie Donna Camp, for buying me the best toys and always taking me to get Ice-Cream by the train tracks. Thank you to my Godie, Wanda Grimsley who loves me a lot and making me a Star Room. Thank you, Auntie Donna Ross for and taking me to McDonalds every time you pick us up.

Dedication

Book dedication communicated exactly as Miss Adira stated: I want to dedicate this book to everyone in all of my family. To Gracelyn who is my best friend forever and forever. She's my baby and she listens to meall the time. To Papa Mango for giving me skittles in his office and sending me texts.

To my Aunt Tina who plays with me and Gracie at the playground, pool and takesus to get Ice-Cream with sprinkles by the train tracks. I love Aunt Tina. Mommy, uncle Denny eyes go small when he smiles.

To Auntie Donna Camp, she plays hide and go seek and I always find her. We play a lot and have fun.

To my Godie for making me a Star Room. My Godie hugs so, so tight Mommy. To my G-Daddy who teaches me basketball with my big brothers, Gabe and Hollis, I beat them. I shoot high with G-Daddy, he lifts me high on his neck, he can do anything big.

To Aunt Sidney in Jacksonville World, she loves me like I love her.

To my MiMi and Pop in Lakeland with the big swing in the backyard. Mimi painted pretty pictures with me.

To my MiMi and Papa in Jacksonville World. I want to see Mimi and Papa, Mommy. I know where Papa keeps his candy and I can get it all the time.

My Nana in Georgia World. Mommy, she hasn't sent me a new text yet. I'm going to send her a unicorn and hearts, she likes them.

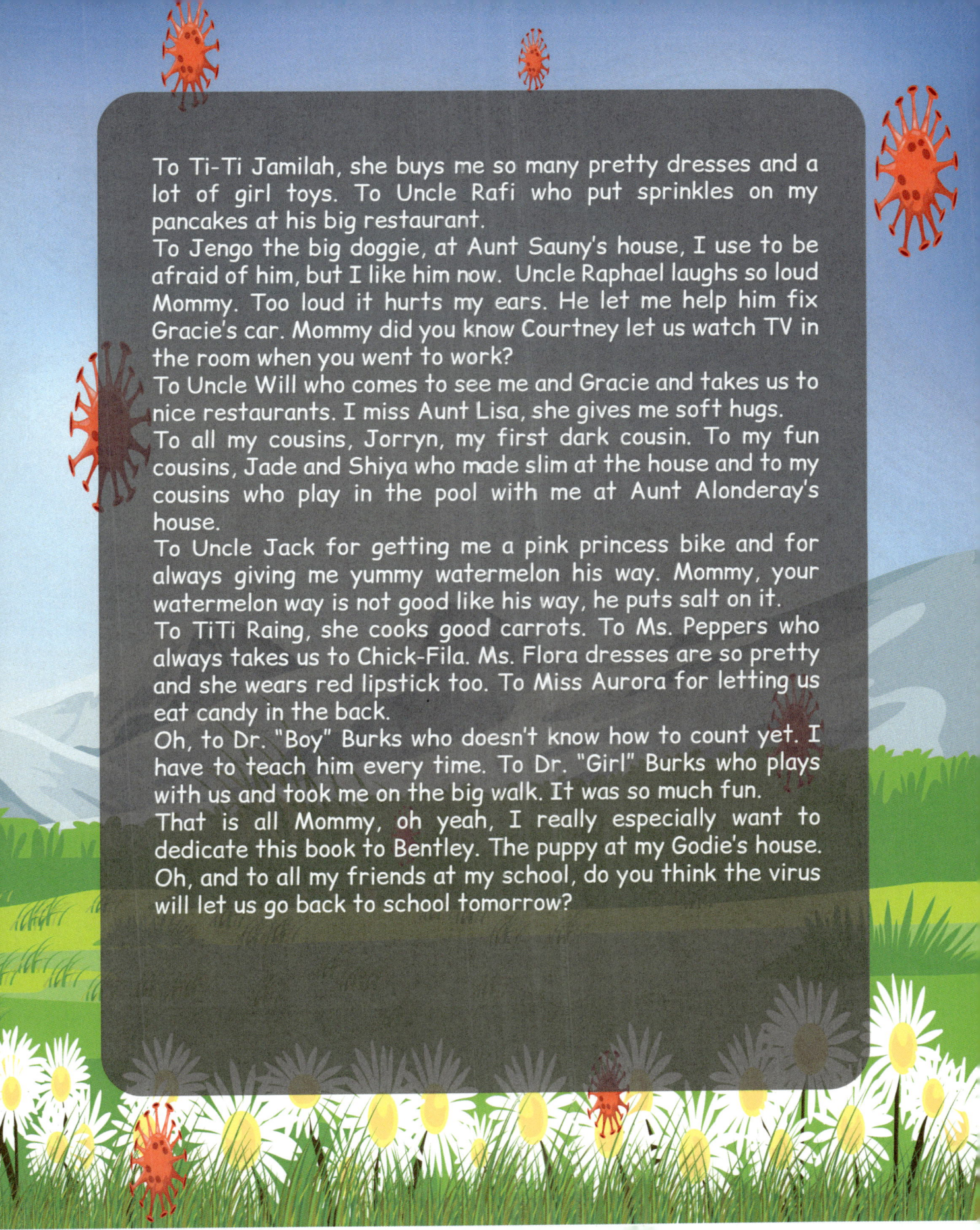

To Ti-Ti Jamilah, she buys me so many pretty dresses and a lot of girl toys. To Uncle Rafi who put sprinkles on my pancakes at his big restaurant.

To Jengo the big doggie, at Aunt Sauny's house, I use to be afraid of him, but I like him now. Uncle Raphael laughs so loud Mommy. Too loud it hurts my ears. He let me help him fix Gracie's car. Mommy did you know Courtney let us watch TV in the room when you went to work?

To Uncle Will who comes to see me and Gracie and takes us to nice restaurants. I miss Aunt Lisa, she gives me soft hugs.

To all my cousins, Jorryn, my first dark cousin. To my fun cousins, Jade and Shiya who made slim at the house and to my cousins who play in the pool with me at Aunt Alonderay's house.

To Uncle Jack for getting me a pink princess bike and for always giving me yummy watermelon his way. Mommy, your watermelon way is not good like his way, he puts salt on it.

To TiTi Raing, she cooks good carrots. To Ms. Peppers who always takes us to Chick-Fila. Ms. Flora dresses are so pretty and she wears red lipstick too. To Miss Aurora for letting us eat candy in the back.

Oh, to Dr. "Boy" Burks who doesn't know how to count yet. I have to teach him every time. To Dr. "Girl" Burks who plays with us and took me on the big walk. It was so much fun.

That is all Mommy, oh yeah, I really especially want to dedicate this book to Bentley. The puppy at my Godie's house. Oh, and to all my friends at my school, do you think the virus will let us go back to school tomorrow?

INTRODUCTION

Congratulations on buying my book, I hope you like it. My book is about my Mommy, my sister Gracie and me when the virus came and took over our regular world and made us stay inside all the time. We lived in the house for a very long time and couldn't go anywhere. The whole World was Sick Outside, so we had to stay inside to be safe. No one could come visit us and we couldn't go visit anyone else. When we did go out we had to wear our mask. At first the mask looked scary to me and my sister Gracelyn, she didn't like them. She cried and would not let Mommy put it on her. My mask was too big but Mommy's teacher friend made us some new ones and it fit perfectly.

In my house it was sometimes fun and sometimes not. My Mommy made us clean up every day. I don't like to put socks together, but I did learn to vacuum the floor. I vacuum my room, the living room and all the rugs in my Mommy's office.

We did a lot of playing and running inside and outside to play to hide and seek. Every day we played outside in the backyard. We worked in the garden, we swam in the pool and I planted my own Sunflowers and beans. My sister planted her some beans too. She wrote too much and made my Mommy angry at her. Sometimes she wrote on the couch and the dresser and even the wall. Mommy was angry at Gracelyn and made her clean it all up. Gracie likes to color and write on everything everywhere. I was angry too because she messed up my pretty room.

The TV always had a lot of talking people, telling about the Pandemic. The President of the United States talked, the Surgeon General talked, the Governor of Florida talked and told us about the virus every day. Every day, they wore church clothes with a tie and talked to us about the virus. We learned what was going on in the world outside of our house by listening to them.

It was so sad, many people died during that time. Mommy says, heaven received a lot of new people, every time a person leaves this earth they go to heaven or to the bad place. On the news, the talking people kept saying how many people died. I wondered, what were they doing in heaven or the other place. At the time of my book thousands of people had already died and we are still stuck in the house. So many people went to heaven but not my family. We did not die and are still alive.

This book will let you see how I lived during the virus. From March to June 2020 I did so many special things. Right now, I'm about to paint in the playroom so I have to go until tomorrow when I tell you more.

I hope when you read my book you will think about people and pray for them too because the world is really sick, and it needs to get well soon.

It was regular day; we went to school had fun with my teacher. Everyone in my class did good in circle time that day. No one got sent to timeout. We talked about the letter H. H is for horse, hamburger, house and hand.

Mommy picked Gracie and me up and we went home. Mommy was not cooking so she said we could pick a place to eat.

I wanted McDonalds and Gracie wanted Popeyes, so Mommy took us to both McDonalds and to Popeyes so she could eat chicken too. We all ate in the car like we sometimes do.

When we got home, we started our Three B's. The three B's are bath, book and bed. This time, Mommy let us watch the TV News with her. She was talking on the phone about the Virus and the people on the TV News was talking about a virus too. They called it a Pandament. I asked mommy what was a Pandament and she said she would tell me later. She didn't have to tell me, I learned on my own.

A Pandament is when people stay home with their families and do not go to stores and school because the world is sick and needs to get medicine. During a Pandament, everyone must stay inside until the world takes its medicine.

Mommy's phone kept ringing a lot about the virus. While Gracie and I fell asleep in Mommy's arms after she read to us.

Did you know that a virus is something that causes people to get really sick and some people die? It's all apart of the Pandament. The next day I learned about the virus because Gracie went to school but my school closed to protect everyone from the virus. I wanted my sister to stay home too but Mommy said, she was okay for that day. The virus had not reached Gracie's school. I was so happy. I love my sister Gracelyn.

It was just me and Mommy, not Gracie. We called it "Mommy and Adira Day" I was bubbly soft on the inside. I love my Mommy. We went to breakfast and ate yummy pancakes. We went for a walk holding hands and talking about blueberry muffins and kittens. Mommy let me sit on her lap in the park and swing high.

Before we picked up Gracelyn from school, we went shopping to buy things for us in the house when the virus came. At the store, it was so many people, I had never seen that many people before. Long lines were all around every lane and some people had wrinkles on their face.

Mommy bought so much stuff, it almost covered my head. I wanted to go home. I wanted to get my sister. I didn't like the store that day. People did not look so happy.

Mommy said, everyone was buying so much because everyone would need to stay inside to and protect ourselves from the virus.

The virus took church away.

We go to church all the time. My mommy is a pastor of a church. A pastor tells good stories to many people. We always go to the church and have to stay there for a long time. Some days we go and play in Mommy's study, or in the children's room.

On Sunday, we dress up and everyone comes to listen to Mommy's storytime, the virus took that away. We couldn't go to church anymore.

The first Sunday it was time for church, we did not get dressed to go to the church, but we stayed and had church at home.

I kept asking Mommy to go, but she said, church was going to be in her office, and we could listen but we had to be quiet.

I kept thinking, how does a Mommy have church in her office?

Can you belief it? The world was so sick, the virus took away my school too.

School was not away from the house anymore. Not only did we do church at home, we even had to do school.

Every morning after breakfast we had school with Ms. M. on Youtube. We loved seeing her every day with the morning train.

After Mommy did her first work on the computer, she gave Gracie and me more school. We went to reading center, music center, art center, cooking station, building station and always outside.

It was always fun though, in Mommy's school, we made green food, we baked vegetable breads. We made up songs and dances with the drums. We learned how to make sun tea in the yard. We had so much fun together.

I even planted beans and sunflowers in a garden we made.

The virus was fun for me and Gracie in our house, but it was mean to the outside world. The Virus made people sick and many people went to heaven if they loved Jesus.

Every day, the Prepdense and Surgiol General and the Govnoor of our state, talked on the TV News. They kept telling us about the people who were sick from the virus and dying.

Mommy said, we needed to pray to God to help people fighting the virus and to pray for their families. The virus was making so many people sad and it was very dangerous just like touching fire. Mommy says, you should never touch fire.

Everyday we prayed for everyone in the world with the virus and for those helping people with the virus. Some of the Doctors even got sick helping others with the virus. The whole world was getting sick.

The virus made us wear mask.

Mommy made sure we were safe, we stayed inside for weeks. When we did go out had to wear mask. At first Gracie feared the mask, she cried and cried and none of them fit. She called everyone she saw, monsters.

Our mask didn't fit our small faces, they would fall off. Then one of Mommy's teacher friends made us special mask. We were so happy. A lady from Mommy's church made us pink masks too. Pink is one of my favorite colors.

Everyone was helping everyone out during the virus, so this church called Tablenapkin Baptist made mask for everyone in the city to come get one. They looked a little scary but they were nice people who also gave us lunch.

Two times we did leave the house and went to visit my family. We always kept handzertizer everywhere. In the house, in the car, at the door, everywhere. So when we got in the car we had to use our handzertizer.

We met them at a park.

We played outside is was so much fun. I could not stop laughing. My cousins took me on the playground, and we played Tennis and my Ti-Ti brought Gracelyn and me tasty snacks and strawberries. Strawberries are my favorite.

I had to use the bathroom, but the virus had taken away outside bathrooms too. Mommy took me behind a tree. I laughed so hard to pee outside behind a tree in the park. That was even fun.

The next time we left the house, we did an Easter Egg hunt in my Auntie's yard. We loved it. So much eating a lot of good food, swimming in the pool, laughing and playing with my other cousins. I even found a golden egg with 10 dollars in it.

Mommy said, that was a special celebration, but we couldn't do it again during the Pandament so we stayed in the rest of the time.

I was so happy I had a hard time falling to sleep that night.

I will never forger the Pandament and I'm so glad the virus didn't make us sick.

The best part about the Pandament and the Virus was having fun with my family. I facetimed all my family. My Nana in Georgia texted me unicorns. My Godie and G-Daddy talked to me on Facetime and sent me videos on Marco Polo. I sang songs to my friends and sent them messages. My papa facetimed sometimes and we laughed on the phone.

We made every Friday movie night and stayed up watching Netflix until everyone fell asleep. Mommy made us popcorn and ice-cream cones.

During the hot days, we made ice-cups, yummy. We had green, purple, pink, red and orange.

The Virus made the world sick but made me very happy.

I don't know how long the Pandament will last, Mommy says I'll be going to a new school when it comes back again. I hope the virus has gone home by then.

I don't want any more people to die.

I want to leave the house without my mask.
I might want to go back to church again one day and I really can't wait to see all my family and friends.

I'm glad we stopped listening to the TV news and started watching Paw Patrols.

I hope people get food in their houses again. The TV News said, mommy's and daddies couldn't work anymore so they don't have food.

I also want to go to X-Ray Fish restaurant again, it is my favorite place to eat.

Huh, I'm ready for the world to take its medicine and get well.

I think I'll just pray and ask
God to make it end.

Made in the USA
Monee, IL
27 July 2020